Mairead is a newly inspired author residing in Ontario, Canada, who enjoys bringing her contemplative thoughts, memories and poetry to others. She has spent her years employed in administrative and secretarial positions, volunteering with deaf and hard of hearing children and adults. She is a mother and grandmother who has learned to live the ups and downs of life while maintaining a deep spiritual connection through her faith.

Mairead hopes her writings will inspire others to pursue their dreams by bringing out the gifts they carry for others to see and appreciate.

With heartfelt love, I thank my family and friends for their continuous encouragement and at times, laughs along the way.

In remembrance of those who have left this world but together with God, helped to grace me with strength, endurance, discernment and a sense of humor.

Mairead

IMPACT

Loving Through Your Eyes

AUSTIN MACAULEY PUBLISHERS®
LONDON • CAMBRIDGE • NEW YORK • SHARJAH

All of the events in this memoir are true to the best of author's memory. The views expressed in this memoir are solely those of the author.

Ordering Information
Quantity sales: Special discounts are available on quantity purchases by corporations, associations, and others. For details, contact the publisher at the address below.

Publisher's Cataloging-in-Publication data
Mairead
Impact

ISBN 9798895430668 (Paperback)
ISBN 9798895430675 (ePub e-book)

Library of Congress Control Number: 2025907451

www.austinmacauley.com/us

First Published 2025
Austin Macauley Publishers LLC
40 Wall Street, 33rd Floor, Suite 3302
New York, NY 10005
USA

mail-usa@austinmacauley.com
+1 (646) 5125767

I would especially like to thank Austin Macauley Publishers for their expertise and by being a welcoming and guiding presence on my journey.

Table of Contents

Chapter 1
Potatoes and Cabbages

Standing on a busy street corner on a hot, humid, downtown Toronto Ontario street, people pass by with their dirty shaking hands held out for money. I scrounged through my pocket for a few coins and willingly put them into their sweaty palms, recalling a conversation in a coffee shop years ago with a homeless guy shabbily dressed. Very eager to make his point, he firmly put down his coffee cup and said, "Not all street people are drug addicts and criminals; we have a story too! Some choose to live outside of the system even though they have had good educations and earned degrees." I sensed immediately he was well-read with an inner peace and more importantly, we cannot always judge a book by its cover!

While glancing off in the distance at the old famous CNE (Canadian National Exhibition), I found myself reflecting to my early childhood and family history. I was making a mental note of how downtown seems the same today as back in 1940s and 50s. I was an only child, barely dressed and reared mainly in poverty (shacked up in dark dingy basement apartments) mainly, meaning one side of the family was quite poor, while the other side was quite wealthy. The poor side and earlier generations emigrated from Catholic Ireland beginning with the Potato Famine; a famine which was not so much about a shortage of potatoes, but opened the door of opportunity for the government in the severe and cruel 1800s, to confiscate farmland or property from citizens, leaving them to starvation while roaming the streets to their death. Some managed to find shelter in caves and workhouses.

These dwellings with row upon rows of beds – men on one side of the building and women and children on the other – offered minimal shelter, food and support. The remainder who had more pennies, boarded ships (sometimes referred to as coffin ships) on a perilous journey to Canada and USA. Many of these Irish immigrants and their families on the ships were ill with Typhoid Fever before arriving at their long-awaited destination, resulting in death. Ships docked on Toronto Lakeshore carrying immigrants with little life lingering in their weak, tired bodies and souls, found themselves in a new land. A spark of hope prevailed in an uncertain future. Today, the Irish Famine Monument is erected at Irish Park on the Toronto shoreline in memory of the 1,186 Irish immigrants. Beautiful sculptures capture the moment in their hearts and gracefully touch the hearts of visitors. Irish Park was in the working, beginning in 1995 and completed in 2007.

As I stood gazing at my mother's Catholic elementary school in Cabbage town, I could almost see her playing in the schoolyard and remembered her telling me how many Irish immigrants settled in the areas named Cabbage town and Corktown. They grew huge cabbages on their front lawns! The aroma of cooked cabbages in homemade Irish recipes filled the air on their streets! Living in poverty didn't stop them from sharing the little they had with others in need. The Catholic Irish were generally not welcomed to apply for jobs, so this made it difficult to rise out of poverty, especially with my Irish grandmother passing away from a long and painful cancer when my mother was only seven years old. I wasn't born yet, but felt proud when my relatives later told me I was just like my Irish grandmother. There were many times, knowing her in this simple comment, that I felt her love and strength which gave me a sense of belonging and missing her. Interesting how I could feel such an attachment to someone, a relative, who died before I ever met them! I was always intrigued that my Irish grandma was raised, for part of her childhood, in a Convent School in Cork County, Ireland, and I still hope to visit there one day. I've enjoyed pictures of blended greens in the hilly countryside and quaint cottages surrounded by colorful dainty flowers.

Children at that time (late 1800s–1900s) were placed in Convent Schools if they were orphaned or if their mother passed away and their father was in the military moving about. I admit, years later knowing what happened in the Indigenous Residential Schools, I wondered *if my Irish grandmother and children in the Convent Schools were ever abused.*

My grandfather, who originated from England, had a disability from a knee injury caused when sliding into a base playing baseball years earlier. Grandpa managed to get a job in a stifling hot hospital boiler room by day and sold needles and thread door to door on the side. It was war time followed by the Great Depression, and times were tough.

My mother said she came to love eating Pobbies – bread and warm milk with sugar.

Humble Soul

A candlelit night for all to pray
Upon their knees at the end of day
Silent words from each broken soul
Drifting up with incense to Heaven's bowl
Now being stirred and mixed from above
Returns to them with fragrance and love
When suddenly amid a crowd he stands
Poor and broken stretches out his hands
While walking toward the spirit unseen
In shabby dress, he moves so serene
Seeming to touch the spirit for grace
Bows his head; wipes a tear from his face
Silent words from his humble soul
Drifting up again to Heaven's bowl

Being stirred, mixed once more from above
Returns only for him with fragrance and love
He felt the presence of spirit so pure
Giving strength and courage to endure
Now turning slowly to end his time
He walked away as he heard the chime
It rings in his heart; only he can hear
Living life in humility, leaves nothing to fear
A humble soul, for this we yearn
In watching him, we will surely learn!

Chapter 2
Auntie's Five

My mother spent a lot of time outside, playing with friends while her older brother was away at war, and her older sister left home for marriage and to start a family. My mother's sister, my auntie, was an example of enormous strength to me growing, up even though we never really shared many conversations on a personal level. It was how life unfolded for her, and how she endured, that I observed closely. Auntie and her hubby were in a state of sheer joy when they were completing their newly built home in the suburbs and expecting their fifth child. Everything was great! So much joy in the blessings they were granted when suddenly her hubby died in surgery from a bleeding ulcer. Getting past this shock and learning to live with it, led my auntie out of the suburbs to start a small dry-cleaning business in a downtown residential area and smaller home with her five children.

Who could believe tragedy and shock would soon come again when a raging house-fire caused from faulty wiring took the lives of auntie's five children – my cousins whose ages were from one-and-a-half to ten years. I was the same age as the ten-year-old. Auntie survived the fire only because the firemen loudly shouted, “Jump out of a window NOW! The floors are caving in, and the house is burning fast!” She frantically tried to walk across the floors to her babies calling out for their mommy, but the floors were weak and did not support her – visions and sounds of that day would leave her with sleepless nights for years to come. As the silence grew around her, she jumped while her life and loves were going up in smoke. She broke her leg, and went to the hospital left with only the pajamas she was wearing. A picture of her with a terrified pale face being lifted into the ambulance was on the front of every local newspaper that evening.

Auntie, who had a wee Irish accent, left-over from her mother, certainly inherited Irish strength and explained to me later that her children went to Heaven to be with their father. I think it was at this time I believed there is a reason and purpose for everything coming from a more powerful source – in good times and bad – and without understanding why, although we may one day. Auntie kept a large box in her basement for many years with letters of heartfelt condolences from all over Canada; mostly people who had tragically lost a loved one in a fire. I was quite young when she gave permission to read the letters, and they left a mark of deep sorrow, mixed with hope and love for the rest of my life.

Today, I still remember my little cousins. I see their faces, hear their playful voices, and find myself easily crying for being without them and wondering who they may have become.

The funeral was very difficult and painful, standing next to my sobbing grandpa. I held his hand to comfort him as we looked upon the tiny caskets placed one on top of the other, placed two on top of two, with the baby casket resting on top. This was the darkest time in our family which left a permanent mark, with unbearable emptiness in our souls.

Love Notes

Love Notes did the spirit bring
To fill my heart so I could sing
North, east, west, south they came
Each to share about the name
Of one they missed as I did too
We're now one – I and you!
Peace and love we did gain
While drowning in the depths of pain
Perhaps our lesson, now was clear
Sorrow, love shared far and near
We are one in our plea
Knowing they have been set free
Gather 'round the candle bright
They're still with us day and night
Healing peace is our cure
Love Notes in a light so pure

*****

Chapter 3
A Wealth of Disappearance

My father's side of the family was a different scene. English and wealthy, they owned several Toronto properties and cars, (a few being antiques) and a beautiful cottage in Muskoka. They were always happy and content, enjoying it all at their own pace. I was included in their lifestyle at special times, such as celebrations and vacations. My father though, never settled or was established. He had a short stint in the Navy and upon returning, his favorite pastime became nightclubs, betting horses and, finally, booze. He let me bet a horse once, and he was more excited than I was when Book Master won – $25.00, which was a lot for a child in those days! This lifestyle made my mother's life a hell, and she could not provide for us alone by working in a bakery. With that Irish determination, she changed jobs and increased her salary enough to make her more independent. She broke away from my father when I was 14 years old and later divorced him. Neither ever re-married. During the separation, I ended up with shingles around my waist, having excruciating pain with weeping sores keeping me out of school for a month and a half. I was exhausted from stress, trying to be whom and what everyone else thought I should be, and all the while living in the chaos of basic survival.

At this point, I never saw the wealthy side of the family again. What I always carried with me was how the poor side of the family rallied 'round offering emotional and financial support while the wealthy side just disappeared. This included grandparents, aunts, uncles, a cousin and my father, slowly drifting out of sight.

During my parent's marriage, there was another fire where all furnishings and my hamster were lost. We were not home though, spending the weekend visiting my aunt.

My wealthy Protestant grandmother was not keen on my mother being Catholic, and when I was born, threatened to take me from my mother if she raised me Catholic, saying, "I have the money to do it!" My mother was very young, still living in poverty and was intimidated by this threat. However, it was only a barking dog. The cold distance between my poor mother and wealthy grandmother was felt by both me and my father. With my father practicing no faith, my mother proceeded to raise me Catholic – quietly. Surprisingly, as life would have it, Catholicism takes a turn in my later years.

I Live Within

I live within where light resides
Gentle breeze deep inside
Warming glow all around
With silence as the only sound
Fresh waters fall to renew
Only felt to imbue
Spirit comes to visit me
I share my gift of poetry
Now to stand upon the earth
I live with spirit in endless mirth!

*****

Chapter 4
Friends, Passing and Marriage

Friends, I had several and with a variety of cultural backgrounds. We all enjoyed sports and later on, school dances. I always felt different, though, like being on the outside looking in. I knew I was liked/loved by my friends and their families; however, the feeling of being on the outside looking in lived deep within me. I dated one guy and after one year of our friendship, he and his best friend died in a car accident. I was to be with them that night at the roller skating rink; however, at the last minute decided to stay at another friend's house for an overnight. This accident, caused by rain, bald tires, and speeding, was terrible for the families. All the school kids, including me, were dazed for months. My boyfriend was impacted by a large tree ripping though the car door and puncturing his lungs; one collapsed and the other on the brink of collapse. His best friend's head hit the steering wheel with such a force that there was a large "V" at the top of the steering wheel. He must have been thrown around the car because the gear shift located in the steering wheel went through his heart. There were no seatbelts in those days. If I had gone on that horrific drive, I would have been sitting in the middle of them – must not have been my time. Sadly, it was theirs. Shortly after the car accident, my grandpa passed away during surgery for a bowel problem. He had asthma and was 75 years old. Obviously it was too much for him, and he went quickly to his destiny.

Time went by quickly, and I fell in love, married and had three children. We had good incomes from steady work, a lovely home with all the toys and trimmings but for good and bad reasons, after 25 years into it, we parted ways and divorced. Good reasons because of the peace, quiet and freedom that came after the divorce and bad reasons because of all that transpired leading up to and during the divorce. Divorce can create many torn feelings of inadequacy and division even when the divorce is wanted. (My marital years could be a book unto itself, however not one that is tied to the thread in this memoir, *Impact*). Once again from stress, I ended up with shingles, although a minor case.

Granny's Balm

Searching here and there for my dear granny
My calls for her to come were many
Others hear my calls, close to me
But wouldn't satisfy to set me free
Oh! Granny appeared all surprised
Happy to see me, let out a big sigh
"What is it my child?" she said in concern
"Tell me, dear lassie, for what do you yearn?"
I fell to my knees; held her apron so tight

Fighting a flood of tears with all my might
"So much hurt; my tummy's a knot"
I said it again and very distraught
She reached in pocket for a lasting cure
That would heal quickly, all for sure
Rubbing my tummy gently with love
I knew there and then, she came from above

Suddenly, one I knew from my past
Wanted to know, "What's wrong with the lass?"
Granny stood firm and pulled me close
Saying, "She's with me now and had her last dose!"
Quickly, the nasty old tyrant went
Knowing what my dear granny meant
I asked Granny, "Now what should I do?"
She said, "Not to worry, there's something for you"
All good, all pure now that you're grown
You will find a balm that's all your own
To place on your tummy or other indeed
From now on will heal you – Go in speed!
Alone in my room, shedding no tear
In most brilliant light, my balm did appear.

*****

Chapter 5
Goodbyes

One thing I was learning about life was to say, "Goodbye" with ease when one is saying it so often. By the grace of God and no matter how many times my heart was broken, it didn't harden me or make me resentful. Instead, I saw lessons to be learned and cherished whatever good could be salvaged to keep any sanity while continuing to love – in relationships, nature, music, helping, sharing, giving, listening, and animals. So many ways to allow love to move and grow! Love had to grow within and around me if I was to live and taking time to ponder alone was important, to reflect and not let life's lessons or the beauty of creation go unnoticed.

Here I will mention nature and how I thought about our beautiful Lake Ontario. When I was young, I went swimming in this lake often with family and friends, only to find one day that a group of politicians decided to use this beautiful lake for dumping sewage and garbage – all in the name of progress. Eventually, the beaches were closed for swimming and freshwater fountains removed. This decision brought serious changes where we now have bottled water from reverse osmosis (separating the good water from the bad.) Sure, it's safe to drink, but it's also dead with no nutrients. The Indigenous knew the damage that would come, but their voices were ignored. What a loss, and we know there are more lakes in trouble. Creation in many ways has been abused and taken for granted. Now we are out of sync, in over our heads, scurrying around looking for solutions.

Four Loves

True, there are four loves each day
"Who are they?" you dare to say
One comes to me, swift and fresh
The other like a heated mesh
Then one so cool and very pure
With one raptured in the final cure
"Who are they?" you dare to say
You've met them all while on your way
Perhaps forgotten during the folly
No, they don't bear a name like Molly
These loves are mine and mine to keep
I'll tell you their names, but not a peep!
Air, the one so swift and fresh
Fire, the one like heated mesh
Water, oh so cool and pure
Earth is one raptured in the cure
Now you want to love them too
Because you know they're here for you!

*****

Chapter 6
Spirit to Suffer

I greatly appreciated the opportunity to travel, especially visiting places with sweeping views of lakes, landscapes, sunrises, sunsets and special historical religious sites that uplifted my spirit.

My thoughts now turned to a very hot humid summer of Covid. I took shelter in my small, air-conditioned apartment and turned on the radio for refreshment, listening to a few old rock tunes, when suddenly it all began with the news announcement that would hit me in the stomach and heart.

Frozen on the spot, I heard the report that 215 unmarked graves were found in Northern Ontario at a residential school – schools planned and established by government leaders and various churches dating back to the 1800s. This wasn't all though! These unmarked graves were in addition to others found previously with more to come that are also located in Canada at residential schools along with years of abuse and neglect of children after they were forcefully torn away from their parents, families and especially mommies. Apparently, years later in the 1980s, the markers for these graves were removed, which was illegal then and is still to this day.

Immediately, I felt a knife shoot through my stomach and heart. I felt the pain and screams of the many Indigenous mothers, grandmothers, families and survivors who were also hearing this horrific news at the same time – Indigenous and non-Indigenous, but connected in the shock and loss of their children.

Tears poured down my face for hours. Nausea in the pit of my stomach with a loss of appetite and 8 lbs. A heavy heart took over my day into the night and following weeks. I saw their little faces every time I closed my eyes. It weighed heavily on my mind that if I felt so sick from this news, how have Indigenous people lived with it for so many generations? I remembered two quotes in the Bible:

"If anyone causes one of these little ones to sin, it will be better if they were thrown into the sea with a millstone around their neck!" (Matthew 18:6).

"Can a Mother forget the Child of her womb?" (Isaiah 49:15)

Well no, she cannot forget! So many questions in the darkness; so few answers! So many injustices; so little changes! Forensics will help enormously regarding disease and abuses in order to fill the gaps for long awaited answers. I could never speak on behalf of Indigenous people, their history and suffering, but I can certainly express the impact of all I was learning and feeling, which includes specific areas of my own history.

I always had a desire to return to former more ancient times for interest, study and worship and the possibilities all opened for me in my later years. Spending a year of studying the history and catechism of the Orthodox Church, for example, brought me to a homecoming while visiting the untainted original worship. Several of my questions and doubts were answered when I learned about the Great Schism 1054 and who left who, in greater detail. 'Was this a waste of my earlier years?' you might ask. No, of course not, because now being more mature, I was ready to take on more and with much more insight. The time arrives and if we are open enough, we know. This applied to all I was learning on so many topics at so many levels and yet all having one thread running through. Surprising and yet not so much, that I would lose a few friends if I made this transition. Sad how a personal decision could make us feel we are on the right path, improving ourselves and still with that, comes losses. Individual life journeys can mean doing it alone at times, so onward. It was very disheartening and impossible, to come to any kind of terms regarding Catholic clergy and the horrific scandals coming out about pedophiles, finances, abuses and cover-ups – in the past and continuing today.

I had loved the religious callings and respected the vocations with such admiration. Now this came crashing down that such evil could infiltrate the Catholic Church and penetrate so many hearts of dedicated families. Of course, I knew this behavior had nothing to do with Christ himself, but I questioned over and over, how could good Catholic clergy, including nuns, permit this in the Church and beyond that, cover it up or promote clergy to other positions and locations? Isn't their vocation to force evil out and let goodness and purity prevail? Aren't they the Door Keepers and Guardians of the Sheep? I knew in my heart that if a system is built on lies and cover-ups, then it will not stand; at least not in the numbers, finances and power it had been enjoying and building up. Eventually, all is exposed for cleansing and will crash to a bare minimum.

Wasn't it Christ who said, "A house divided against itself will not stand?" (Mark 3:25) What Bible were these so-called Catholic Christians reading and following? (Sounds like Hellions) With so many dark corners in the Catholic Church, one just knows to keep your mouth closed, especially in religious communities.

It Is Done

Deep into His Passion; deep into my soul
Now is the time! Commit to be whole
Sad that it is, my will did part
'Twas my beginning carried deep in my heart
As sunrise came and sunset went
Year after year, I lived duty lent
Oh! How I strived to make amends
While keeping up with all the trends
How can I forget the pains He bore?
To save and brighten my soul once more?

A final touch, a final grace
I look deep in my heart to find His face
All bloodied with love from pure divine
Now I am His and He is mine
Hearts in Truth we live as One
He called my will – It is done!

*****

Chapter 7
Broken Hearts at Bedtime

There was a mountain of support and consolation in our family loss, but what kind of support and consolation did the Indigenous receive in their loss? Children were not allowed to return to families even when they were ill, abused or died! Parents (not all) had very limited visits and were not invited to participate in Residential Schools as volunteers. If they questioned or interfered, they were threatened with jail. My little cousins were in their own homes and beds with their mommy nearby when they passed away lost in smoke and fire.

Pain and sorrow welled up inside me, especially when I thought of the broken hearts so many children carried all day long and into the night, living in strange places with people who denied their culture, language and very existence. Even their little prayers taught to them by mommy and daddy at home were silenced, while their hearts cried out in mixed fear and hope that Mommy and Daddy would come soon to take them home. Several children ran away successfully while others were caught and forced to return to the school. I shivered at the thought of these cold, damp schools having a cold environment, food and spirit.

Presentations by Indigenous survivors confirmed my dreaded thoughts in what I was beginning to learn about history and the magnitude of it all. Culture can stay dormant within the deepest recesses of our souls, but eventually the culture surfaces again! With a growing enthusiasm and driving force within, I was looking forward to learning more about Indigenous culture.

Mary's Pen

Her children were lost with nowhere to look
For a path clear and true alongside a brook
Where fresh waters run, and woods smell green
Where nothing is hidden, but all is seen
She stoops down in all her splendor and grace
To touch each of her children upon their sweet face
She pulls out of her pouch, a sparkling pen
And says, "Now it's time for me to begin
I'll write a new story on your hearts today
So, return to the path without delay
Don't look back; be healed be true
To the One who waits in love for you"
Her children smiled and gave her a hug
Now they were safe, warm and snug
Enlightened with wisdom on the path with a song
Forgetting all that went so wrong
Instead, they danced when they thought of her
Mary, who came and loved as they were.

Chapter 8
Keep Your Chin Up!

We tend to dote on our sorrows and heavy hearts, so when a brighter path opens up, better to get on it and learn what awaits us!

I was dabbling and learning so much, however knew there was still more to come.

Several Indigenous websites delighted me with their communities and willingness to share information and answer questions. Late at night, I began a routine of peacefully falling asleep between soft Irish Celtic music and smooth Native flutes with crackling fires.

I grinned at the Irish custom of St Patrick's Day with green beer, storytelling, singing, Shamrocks and then the sweetness of Indigenous birthday parties for children. The child gives his/her invited relatives a special chosen little gift; the relatives don't give a gift in return because it teaches the child about giving and in simplicity. What a lovely tradition continued today, although may not be a tradition in all tribes.

After a little break, I returned to learn about Treaties. This was another rude awakening for me about Treaties that were not signed, sealed and delivered in complete understanding or agreement. It led to the belief of deception with an enormous amount of lost or stolen land, farms and their survival animal, the buffalo; a special animal spiritually gifted to the Indigenous to use for clothing, tipis and food. All was lost now as they were being pushed back more and more with passing time; pushed back – but not to disappear!

The Irish also lost their land, farms and animals, such as sheep. I went through a period in my life when I considered a small piece of land in the country with adorable sheep.

I wouldn't have used their wool but kept them for pets! They are very cute and loveable. Animals for pets is different than animals for survival. The Irish are well-known for their beautiful woolens and knitted clothing, having specific patterns for different counties and clans. There are great informative websites directly from Ireland with these homemade products and educational information about them.

Hey, wait a minute! I thought, *If Indigenous Treaties still exist that are not legitimately signed, sealed and delivered, does this mean I am living on Indigenous land? Wow! This is a lot to ponder!*

A flashback suddenly came of my own divorce settlement and how losing my home I never forgot the happier memories in the family home, including flowers and bushes I planted or taught my little ones to plant a flower in the garden. Cash settlements don't compensate or erase these memories. We just learn to live with the losses. They are part of our personal history as well as part of world history in the space of time. If we willingly give it up, so be it, but by force, cruelty or deception, it leaves a degrading mark; a darkness in history and a darkness in souls. Suddenly I'm reminded Truth begets Truth and Lies beget Lies – or Light vs darkness.

All Comes Forth

How did it leave us? Where did it go?
Is this why we're so empty and low?
The space is there deep down inside
But it seems as though something did hide

Day after day, we were limping along
Waiting for a beautiful song
One that's heard in the depths of our hearts
One that stays and never parts
New wind and fire will gently come
With cleansing all will begin to hum
To wake us up, fill us up, rejoice again
In peace and love, forever then
Softly the song within comes alive
Love in beauty and chorus to thrive
We hold our ground, remaining firm
Angels dream while candles burn
All comes forth to enlighten us now
All comes forth to raise us how?
'Twas Spirit who heard all our cries
And gently dispersed them in the skies
Never will this happen again
That we will separate from the Great Amen!

*****

Chapter 9
Learning to Get Closer

The driving force within me to continue learning did not ease up at all. I spent my days on the internet watching documentaries, movies, presentations, herbs, and homemade recipes such as *Three Sisters Soup, Succotash Stew* and *Fried Bread,* rituals (my favorite being the newborn cedar bath), music, clothing such as pretty ribbon skirts, moccasins, jewelry and finally powwows and smudging.

My spirituality soared when I learned about the White Buffalo Woman, who seemed akin to the Blessed Mother appearing to Catholics and Orthodox in apparitions to bring a message or teaching and in the appearance of the culture she is visiting.

With the Sacred Pipe, Dream Catchers, and Spirit Animals, my respect for nature grew, having a clearer understanding of connection and oneness. I forgot for years that trees give us oxygen! Now a deeper understanding was beginning. It's not about me in the house and the trees and animals outside. It's about me, the trees and animals being here on the land together in creation on Earth with a purpose and connection that makes one see differently as well as see more clearly.

Through an Indigenous presentation, a young man in Northern Ontario, very knowledgeable about herbs and plants, explained when he sees a certain tree change its needles to yellow, he knows it's time for the fish to rise to the top of the lake, and this is when the fish would have the most oil. Enthusiastically, his community prepares to catch an abundance of fish for eating and medicine.

This was so interesting to learn how it all connected from the tree to the table and the perfect timing! How many of us would be sitting in a drifting boat at the wrong time waiting for a fish to catch, without knowing the purpose or doing it mostly for sport. I also discovered colors in a more fervent way, inside and outside the home and for clothing.

Wandering to Irish educational websites on occasion too, I found from my early family roots, there are similarities; the enduring painful history mixed with beautiful linens, tartans, dancing and music, recipes and herbs. Similar, but each being unique in their own intimate culture.

One Spirit

One in Spirit! One in all!
Spirit comes to save our fall
Love apart we cannot do
But love in One if to renew
What's your worry? Why forlorn?
We don't care about human scorn
One in Spirit; One in love
Is how we live in realms above

Above, around us, side to side
We all encompass One inside
With few words we know the other
To understand as One, we'd druther
Oneness permeates all around
Through each heart and to the ground
No longer are we far apart
We've healed division in our heart
One in Spirit; One in love
In One Spirit; in One love.

*****

Chapter 10
Indigenous Acquaintance

I've known a few Indigenous people from a variety of settings. In viewing a video presentation by a young Indigenous woman recently, I learned that she and others, long ago and not so long ago, were cautioned by family to hide language and culture or they might not be eligible to apply for employment or just plain be accepted in society. Others who could pretend they were from various other cultures, did so and were accepted with more ease. So much locked up in their heavy hearts just trying to survive.

In terms of Indigenous culture and history, the topic never came up in the conversations I was having. I never thought anything of it because I was never properly made aware of Indigenous history. Hearing a comment that the Indigenous wanted to live on reserves attending their own schools, to me seemed everyone was happy! So as for the details, I didn't know. Living far from these schools growing up and because the causes and issues were in the media only briefly, on top of nothing being taught in the education system, I and probably many others, missed a lot that was going on. My marriage, family and job kept me knee-deep in other concerns, although I did manage to volunteer time to the marginalized deaf community who also endured a cruel history struggling to survive and find ways to have their needs met. In fact, a deaf man gave me a book to read titled, *Mask of Benevolence* by: Harlan Lane 1999, in hopes I would learn more of their history. Well, I was absolutely stunned to learn there was a plan from those 1800s to put deaf men on an island to castrate them so they couldn't procreate. Thank God that horrible plan fell through!

The deaf have come a long way and are now more visible in education and society. In all that I was learning now, I was very disappointed I didn't know more of the facts earlier in my life. Having said that, better late than never; there is a time and place for everything. The lid is coming off the garbage; truth prevails; darkness into light – all these words fit the cause where now it's in our face daily and should be. Questions are beginning to get responses. Culture is beginning to surface from the deep recesses of Indigenous souls and may I say, all souls, because now more people are searching into their personal histories and cultures properly and thoroughly.

One of my Indigenous acquaintances is dearer to me than others, and it's because a magnet draws me to him, feeling more open to ask questions and share more personally.

Since I heard the sordid news announcement of the unmarked graves, this dear person had been on my worried mind with tears pouring down. Questions I asked myself were, 'How is he or his family taking all this ongoing heart wrenching news? Are there any survivors of Residential Schools in his family? Are they safe? Are they strong?' I was sure he was strong though, because speaking with him once, I suddenly had an experience of feeling his spirit, as if I was suspended in time. His spirit was very big, strong and powerful. I knew immediately his spirit was strong because of what he and his people endured for generations. I was accustomed to spiritual experiences, so wasn't surprised but quickly decided it was best to keep it to myself. He was always very kind and spoke with such calm and patience when we met up with each other. I never asked where he lived but the curiosity was there.

We shared in a simple, comfortable way, questions and comments about each other's lives, families, cultural history and current events. The inner pain he carried was visible at times through the quiet serious moments in our chats. He always contemplated a little before he spoke, which left me in awe. We were serious and yet at times shared warm laughter. I told him how much I had been learning about his people and his big, warm, very dark eyes widened. With a somewhat shy smile, he encouraged me to continue.

Last encounter when sitting close to each other talking softly in a down to earth way, I could look out far, near and all around for my mind to capture at once, all the experiences of joys and sorrows our ancestors had lived. Yes, there was some joy; joys and sorrows that continue in our lives, one way or another today. Learning the same of him, it came together all encompassed in the Creator – our Creator. My heart knew we bonded as friends, sharing so much in common now. Peace and love ran deep within my soul and while we didn't speak those words, I knew we broke through a barrier. Now there was a healing and understanding – a complete trust in a beautiful silent moment that brought us together, knowing life is real and loving through your eyes can be real too! We both had times in our lives of being on the outside looking in; however, now we are on the inside together, looking out.

In Flight

Spirit, I share my heart with you
Under golden sun and sky of blue
Carried away in bright burning flame
Among shining stars and washed in rain
Where time will erase; Spirit becomes light
Filled with love, my heart takes flight
Sweet perfumed flowers; songbirds with me
Come to a garden that says I am free

Free to give; free to love
Free to know the One above
In endless space where there is no time
No effort now to make the climb
Love is here, as is there
Will live eternal – when we care.

*****

Chapter 11
Beauty and Love

A beautiful part of learning about creation and nature, is that it is a gift belonging to everyone. However, the Indigenous haven't forgotten that, especially if living with and in country surroundings away from concrete, competitive cities. This awareness lives in their soul with deep meaning and purpose. Animals, trees, lakes, fish, sky, mountains, stars, moon, fire, water, and air are all connected to people – to us! Too bad so many of us have forgotten to notice in order to preserve and have a sense of well-being! Are we void of respect and cherishing the gift of Creation and Nature? I wondered how many people in *Canada know that many lakes, cities and towns have Indigenous names*. The colonist map of Canada has been tossed out bringing in the new Canadian Atlas now including and showing Indigenous owned land and their specific locations. What an accomplishment! Visit the website to view the new map of Canada for more Indigenous history at: climateatlas.ca

Now I wasn't just seeing, but loving through Indigenous and Irish eyes; all the beauty, natural meaning and purpose with nothing missing. Where does one go for a retreat? One leaves all at home to escape and travel straight away to quiet country surroundings, walking on green and wooded trails perhaps gazing upon an elegant deer, touching flowers and connecting with tiny squirrels, birds and bunnies. This is where and when we contemplate deep within our souls, looking for answers and ultimately peace. How blessed Indigenous are to live day to day, life in such beauty, just being and appreciating, surviving as the creator intended! I experienced a little taste of this way of life when kayaking and camping at Manitoulin Island (Manitoulin means Spirit of the Land) absorbing the beauty and paddling in fresh calm water. Last stop to buy a colorful beaded souvenir.

Clean water is not in all living conditions and is another mountain of stress and grief for Indigenous with little help forthcoming. My heart just dropped during an episode of contaminated water up North on Indigenous land and bottled water was shipped to them immediately by Government according to local News – costing the Indigenous $9-11.00 per bottle and $40.00 per case! No drinking water, no bathing/hygiene, living in poverty and $9-11.00 per bottle. Well, it's crystal clear to me that no efforts to cleanse contaminated lakes and wells could ever be possible until hearts and minds are cleansed first. The layers of delays, cover-ups and brushoffs must be peeled off with new water systems being put into effect. No more quick and temporary fixes!

Believing we are all connected in Creation and Nature as brothers and sisters, the pain, suffering, sorrow and rejection can rise to slip away and turn into a clear pure love. We only need to take time to look through another's eyes to see them and ourselves there together; not apart.

Orange Shirt Day is a memorial for the many sufferings of Indigenous people whether missing, alive or deceased, torn from families, loss of culture and means of survival.

We've known since the beginning of time not to take children from their families, especially their mommies. It is also an uplifting day of hearing stories so hope and healing can prevail. Hanging Orange Ribbons on the fence at City Hall left a calm, prayerful spirit and those listening for the first time, were personally touched and educated. One survivor of Residential School spoke of a teacher who told her she had no soul and when she later asked her father, he said, "If we had no soul, there wouldn't be a word for it!" I never doubted the presence of a soul and thought the teacher's comment was rude and demoralizing – to a defenseless child especially.

I was happy to locate both Indigenous and Irish websites to translate the English word soul to Cree and Irish languages which have several dialects. Soul in Cree is *Ahcahk* (sounds like Achock) and soul in Irish is *Anam*. Interestingly, there are different words for it and yet our Soul, *Ahcahk* and *Anam* are full of the same joys and sorrows from different places in time, of experiences and a deep brokenness, longing for healing, justice, peace and love.

Oral storytelling for Indigenous is an important way of life and the Irish have this custom as well. After all the stories I heard from the Irish about Leprechauns, I felt joy to learn the Indigenous have stories about the Little People! Apparently, the Leprechauns and Little People have very similar behaviors; sometimes kind and giving and other times a little mischievous. If we think about it, we will soon realize that if storytelling, traditions and customs are dropped completely, we will become cultureless mechanical beings living who and what we really are not, with nothing to hand on to our children! We have a responsibility to keep their souls alive and rich in the fullness of their culture.

Lands Near and Far

Birds on high and birds in trees
From near and far, come sit with me
In my wee yard I hear their chatter
For hours I sit; it doesn't matter
Just to hear their words the same
They're just wee birds without a name
All speak the same in one voice
It might be better when there is no choice
From dawn to noon, I watch and listen
When building nests, they have a glisten

These birdies are all one with us
Sharing a language of love and trust
They take a nap or fly away
Then return the very next day
To be the little nameless birds
Chattering away their musical words
When they jump close to stare at me
I stare right back and what I see
Creator's life is all around
Now it's time to touch the ground

Humbled as to who we are
This is for lands near and far
We are One, and now can go
Surprise! Tree gracefully gives a show!

*****

Chapter 12
Truth and Reconciliation, Anyone?

National Truth and Reconciliation Day is commemorated on September 30th in Canada and really is about more than sympathy with dry apologies and having a little truth exposed. I would say all certainly must be exposed and as dark as it may be, it is truth being uncovered and allowed to permeate its brilliant pure light.

Only when we can become humble enough to cry another's tears as we cry our own, will we have empathy and come to love through their eyes, where we finally reach serious Truth and Reconciliation – individually and collectively, ultimately healing wounds to close.

The wounds are so many and very deep and we've all experienced some or all of these wounds at different times in big and small ways – rejection, misunderstanding, deception, poverty, cruelty, loss of family/friends and property, isolation, fear, loneliness, intimidation, illness, low self-esteem, senseless wars, and injustices. Here's the good news! Healing, Truth and Reconciliation can be turned into love, joy and inner peace.

The world is a beautiful garden if we take care of it and one another. Then the garden will take care of us when we are finally loving through the Creator's eyes!

Creator's Will

LOVING THROUGH YOUR EYES
THERE IS NO DISGUISE

TO GET THROUGH WITH PAIN
THE WALLS THAT BLOCK AND MAIM

FREES THE SPIRIT AN OPEN PATH
WE TOSS OUT ALL OUR DOUBT AND WRATH

YOU FEEL THE DEEPEST ME, AND I YOU
TO SEE AS ONE; OUR LOVE GIVES NEW

ONE IN EACH OTHER WHERE FREEDOM LIVES…

SING, DANCE, LET JOY COME IN
NOW DARE WE TOGETHER SHARE A WIN

FOR ALL ETERNITY, NONE CAN KILL
OUR SPIRITS IN CREATOR'S WILL!

*****

Let's Go Forward!

Now that we have looked back into our personal lives and family history, reliving our differences and sorrows, we understand that these tragedies with injustices continue today in a variety of ways. We see it all around us.

This brings us to a point of healing and peace, to be aware that others experience suffering and isolation. We are not alone and never were. What can we do to move forward? We cannot, nor would it be healthy in body, mind and soul to stay in a place mentally, that hurt and/or traps us in our past.

If we are strong enough to overcome (as many are not), and we choose not to overlook situations around us, we can help whether actively or prayerfully. Our hands are not tied as much as we think.

We can donate money directly to causes if we notice corruption in organizations. We can donate time in Soup Kitchens, Shelters, Places of Worship, Food Banks or being a good neighbor and simple sharing. We can say a kind and uplifting word. We can give a hug. We can send a lonely, elderly or ill person a card and perhaps a hand-written note using our own words. We can pick a flower from our garden and put it in their hands. We can share stories and have a tea/coffee together. We can pass on a good book or enjoyable movie and music CD. How about a short meaningful scenic walk together or an invite to a social if we know the person well enough. The ways are endless…

When we have connected hearts with another in their crisis, we have broken great barriers. A new bond has been created. This is not necessarily just between people in a physical presence but includes those who may leave or be at a distance. How is this done? First by touching hearts in our shared experience, then keep the person within us – in our soul. We can remember them perhaps on a special date, place or time of year. We can also be reminded of them at our place of worship and light a candle if that is available. We can include them in our prayer – of going forward. They can be near us too on the other side of the globe! Through the shared experience, bond, healing and awareness, there is spiritual connection. There is love; a love with its source in God/Creator.

We use discernment and good safe sense in helping those around us. They may not want or appreciate the help, however offering is a kind measure bringing many graces for both involved. At times it may seem like it is all give and no take – bear with it in prayer.

I always find it interesting when suddenly someone is put in my path having a need I can meet, or a need of mine that they can meet. The spirit provides – we just need to be open and see! We see with our eyes and we see with our hearts! I remember for approximately two years of my life, almost every stranger approaching me on the street and sometimes inside buildings needed directions. Something so simple and yet profound! I've also had many other experiences making me aware the spirit was involved.

We are all in company of our own guardian angel, and I'm convinced they work together to help us find one another in our time of need, big or small. I thank my guardian angel every day, keeping in mind that they are with us 24/7.

Letting go of disappointments, abuses and painful tragedies we lived through, does not mean we ignore those happenings. We are not doormats and we don't shelve our problems. We do, however, move on with a different vision and plan. We have learned, grown and are maturing in age, mentally and spiritually.

We may decide to speak up by writing letters or protesting for a specific cause closest to our hearts. This would be a cause we connect to naturally because we experienced it ourselves. We will have more passion for the cause – passion meaning heartfelt, not violence.

Forgiving at times seems like such an unfair and impossible thing to bring ourselves to do. We must pray to sincerely forgive and try to consider the other person may be mentally unstable, ignorant of education, or living and working in corruption. These are souls in pain and darkness too. By forgiving, if just in our own hearts, we will heal easier and the other may learn. Some circumstances are just so painful, they are unforgivable. My heart has been there and it is a difficult place to leave in our mind and heart. It does take time, sometimes many years but also continuous prayer. The result for me was that I forgave but did not forget. What does that mean? Well, I genuinely forgave and moved on, but never forgot so I would not allow that into my life again. It became very clear to me that our choices are so very important and have long-lasting effects. We are free to make choices, but consequences do come and sometimes very hard and fast. In short, I forgive but cannot hang out or live in a way that might be expected. Going down a road once can be enough, so choices need to be prayed about, discerned as much as possible either alone or with the help of another more experienced. There comes a time if we want to feel better, heal and mature, we take healthy steps to seek and get on a better path. We need not feel embarrassed or ashamed because we know now others have had to seek out help and guidance whether professionally or a friend/mentor.

It was an enlightenment for me when learning about history, that these terrible things happened all through history and are happening now in the present and will continue in future. The only way to stop it if we cannot change leadership or circumstances around us, is to change ourselves!

It will have an impact on our life as well as lives around us and we will look through another's eyes leaving us to bond and heal, but also gain wisdom, strength and courage to move forward.

In the Spirit of Love,
Mairead

Three Saints

Three saints that came to mind while I was writing this manuscript and poetry, are well-known and well loved by several faith and cultural communities around the world. It is good to learn about these saints because they were everyday human beings just like you and I. They lived in difficult times and they endured in prayer and suffering while their spiritual lives soared to great heights. In their life and death, we were left wonderful teachings to help us on our journey. Many have turned to their readings to gain more insight into a prayer life and mostly how to be strong in our trials, not giving up hope and trust in God our creator who loves us unconditionally, but also in our weaknesses. These saints and more are examples for us in whatever way they touch our hearts.

SAINT TERESA OF AVILA – DECLARED DOCTOR OF THE CHURCH 1970, CELEBRATED OCT 15–Saint Teresa of Avila was born March 28, 1515 and died October 4, 1582. She was a Spanish mystic whose desire was to begin the reform of the Carmelite Order and return it to the Primitive Life and Rule, as it was first founded. She lived in Avila Spain and within two years of entering Religious Life, she collapsed and became an invalid for three years.

During her time of illness, she became more interested in prayer and meditation. After her recovery, she spent 15 years divided in worldly and divine spirit and suddenly had a religious awakening in 1555.

Teresa never gave up on her calling to reform the Carmelite Order returning it to the Primitive Rule. She was met with much opposition however persevered, travelling hundreds of miles and mostly in sickness. At one point, during bad weather and hardship on her travels in horse drawn wagons, she cried out to God, "If this is how you treat your friends, no wonder you have so few!"

Carmelites are a cloistered monastic order and while the cloister seems to be the ultimate goal for anyone desiring a vocation inside the cloister, Teresa was only inside the cloister for eight years and more often outside, ill, facing opposition and threats mainly from clergy. During these times, she would be relying heavily on charity from others who were supportive of her mission. They would give her food and shelter until she moved on again.

Teresa gave up on prayer for a long time, however when she had her religious awakening, she persevered more fervently. She founded more than 16 convents and with this, disputes and imprisonments took place between the Carmelite Friars who wanted the Primitive Rule and those who did not. Teresa kept going. Teresa kept praying.

Teresa endured much more than this. However, the point here is the level of suffering for one woman who wanted to simply return to a Primitive Rule with enough people interested to agree. I'm sure at times she felt quite abandoned by God, whom she trusted and loved so much.

She would have also felt abandoned by clergy who were not supportive or willing to listen and assist. She was very much alone in her quest. Holding fast to the belief in her mission, she accomplished her work for God and the Carmelite Order. This left her with a prayer life so beyond most of us however her books are available for us to read and learn. They are available in most bookstores and on the internet now. Both the Carmelites of the Primitive Rule and Old Rule, still exist today. Teresa's books for inspiration in our prayer life to mention a few are – *The Interior Castle, The Way of Perfection* and *Conceptions on the Love of God.*

*****

SAINT KATERI TEKAKWITHA, FIRST INDIGENOUS SAINT CELEBRATED JULY 14–Saint Kateri known as "Lily of the Mohawks" is patroness of ecology and the environment. She was born to a Mohawk Chief and Christian Algonquin woman in 1656. With Small Pox being rampant, Kateri lost her parents and brother when she was four years old, leaving her an orphan. She later contracted Small Pox but recovered. However, she was left with impaired vision and permanent scars on her face.

Kateri was raised by her uncle, who became the Mohawk Chief, and she was taught Christianity living with the Mohawk Tribe. She was baptized in 1676 by a Jesuit Missionary. Kateri became a devoted Christian and by age 19 took a vow of chastity. While many were inspired by her exemplary piety, others were harassing her and even becoming hostile.

Living in this environment became too difficult and

Kateri decided to move to a settlement in Canada which is now known as Montreal. She travelled by foot from New York up to Canada to escape to a place where she could live her faith and Christian life. Her faith grew, and she lived a life of prayer and penance. Her zeal was admired by many.

Only five years later, Kateri passed away at age 24 on April 17, 1680. Her last words were "Jesus, I love you." It is written that when she passed away, she was surrounded by those who loved her and they saw her face clear of all Small Pox scars and glowing.

Saint Kateri was exemplary in her steadfast faith and endurance. She was separated from her dear family at a tender age of four, later escaping to another country on foot, resulting in her death at age 24. She is loved and admired by both Indigenous and other cultures who visit her shrines in Auriesville, NY and Montreal, Canada.

Kateri is a different example left for us in that she was graced at a very young age to endure what was to come. A quiet and gentle soul who, by grace, endured all she had to. Her zeal for her faith, committed prayer life and heroic suffering are left for us to learn more about Kateri. I hope Saint Kateri touches your heart as she has touched mine and many others! Books for Saint Kateri (Lily of the Mohawks) are many and to mention a few – *Saint Kateri Lily of the Mohawks, Saint Kateri Model of Bravery,* and *Saint Kateri Tekakwitha*. Try Amazon or a bookstore for purchasing. Note: Kateri is Catherine in English and the name she was given at her baptism.

*****

SAINT FRANCIS OF ASSISI, STIGMATIST CELEBRATED ON OCTOBER 4– Saint Francis was born 1181/82 in Spoleto Italy and died October 3, 1226 in Assisi, Italy. He was canonized July 16, 1228 being founder of the Franciscan Order (Friars) Poor Clares (Nuns) and Third Order (laity.) Francis' zeal was for poverty, penance and charity. His personal charisma drew thousands to follow him into this way of life. He was called the 'Poor Little Man' as he strived and endured many hardships to follow Christ as closely as possible. He is one of the most venerated saints in the Catholic history, but also venerated in several other faith communities. He is the Patron Saint of Italy and of Ecology.

Saint Francis had such a love and connection to animals that they adored him, knelt down and became tame from wild by the touch of his hand or gaze into their eyes. The custom is not just in Italy, but around the world for people to have their pets and farm animals, sick or well, blessed at their local Church in remembrance of St. Francis and his love for animals. He was one with nature.

Francis suffered dearly, walking miles in dry heat with sun bearing down on him. This caused him to have serious vision problems. He wore an old piece of cloth for his religious garb/clothing and cloth shoes. These are kept in the Bascilica in Assisi for viewing. Saint Francis was devoted to reading the Passion of Christ – the days leading up to His crucifixion and eventually with his prayer and penance living in poverty, he showed signs of bearing the Stigmata, which are the wounds of Christ.

There are a few interesting points about Francis' life before being called to serve God. He was in the army fighting a battle, however heard God speak to him and felt compelled to turn away from war and bearing arms. To this day, Franciscans, including Lay Franciscans, will not bear arms or enter into war. Francis was also expected by his father to take over the well-established textile business and when Francis left the military, his father was shamed. Francis eventually told his father that he did not want the role of being a textile merchant and instead felt called by God to serve God. His father was enraged and disowned Francis. The mother was broken-hearted knowing and understanding her son in a deeper way.

One day in the square in Assisi, Francis disrobed to show he renounced the ways and riches of the world in order to follow Christ. The bishop was present and wrapped a garment around Francis, accepting him as one of his own. Sad to say, Francis ended up in a prison where he was starved and became very ill, almost to the point of death. He was released though and continued with his calling. He permanently left home to live his life of poverty according to Christ and the Gospels. After his followers had increased in size, he founded the Orders and went about preaching as a deacon. He never became a priest. He begged for food and anything else he might need. He lived on the verge of nothingness always.

Francis had a strong distaste for lepers prior to his calling to follow Christ however after his calling, he saw a leper one day and went over to him and hugged him tightly, feeling no fear and no shame. Lepers were shunned by the rest of the community, but Francis would not do this any longer. He was a new man in Christ and held to his convictions.

At this time in history, there was a rift with Muslims and Francis challenged danger and went to visit the Sultan. Surprisingly, the Sultan welcomed him, and they spoke at great length – about peace. The Sultan liked Francis and they shared much in common. Francis later said the Sultan wanted peace as much as he did. Francis returned to his community, exhausted from the journey and in poor health.

There was a time when his Friars in community started to bring in books and fancy dishes, bowls of decorative fruit etc., and this disappointed Francis very much. He said they were not following the 'Rule of Life' as was written by him but also approved by the Pope at that time – Honorarius. Francis left the community he was living with and with a few who agreed with him, they went to live elsewhere – in a cave.

Saint Francis was small in stature, frail in health, going blind and becoming increasingly weak. The few friars stayed close by to watch over him and provide care. He died a beautiful and holy death. His Franciscan Orders all exist today in their different charisms and constitutions. There remains today, the original Franciscans Minor as Francis founded.

Learning about Saint Francis of Assisi is different again from other Saints mentioned here, but we can understand how he changed when God called him and how he responded with great conviction and even left his father's business and house to follow his conviction.

Saint Francis was and still is a very loved and admired Saint for his life of poverty, faithfully living the Gospels and keeping the Rule of Life he wrote and was approved by the Pope. Many pilgrims of all faiths visit Assisi to pay homage to this Saint and pray for his intercession. Assisi is a very peaceful place that even the white doves aren't chased away when people come close!

There are numerous books about Saint Francis of Assisi and to mention a few – *St. Francis of Assisi Biography, Prayer of St. Francis,* and *Day by Day with St. Francis.* These and other books can be found on Amazon or in bookstores. Readers will be happy to learn about Saint Francis of Assisi and begin to follow his way of simplicity, love for the poor and ecology/animals. Here is a well-known hymn written about Saint Francis…

Make Me A Channel of Your Peace

Make me a channel of your peace
Where there is hatred, let me bring your love
Where there is injury, your healing power
And where there's doubt, true faith in you.
Make me a channel of your peace
Where there's despair in life let me bring hope
Where there is darkness, only light,
And where there's sadness, ever joy.
O spirit, grant that I may never seek
So much to be consoled as to console
To be understood as to understand,
To be loved as to love with all my soul.
Make me a channel of your peace
It is in pardoning that we are pardoned,
In giving to all that we receive,
And in dying we're born to eternal life.
(taken from hymnary.org)

*****

Sources

*HISTORY OF POTATO FAMINE – Ch. 1
Effects on the People of Ireland
Escaping to Canada
Youtube: Irish in Canada
Website: https://canadairelandfoundation.com
See: Ireland Park

The Great Irish Famine – Documentary 1996
Youtube: Vintage Broadcasting System

Ireland's Great Hunger and the Irish Diaspora
Youtube: Rebecca Abbot

Corktown History of a Toronto Neighborhood
Youtube: Corktown Lane TV

TREATY NO. 1 – Ch. 8
Youtube: 2020 Anishnaabe History Podcast
Youtube: City of Winnipeg 150 Anniversary
Youtube: CBC Docs

TREATY NO. 13 – Ch. 8
Youtube: Treaties Recognition Week (1805)
Youtube: Mississaugas of the Credit First Nation
Youtube: Oakville & Historical Society

RESIDENTIAL SCHOOLS – Ch. 6,7,10,12
Crimes Against Children at Residential School:
The Truth about St. Anne's
Youtube: The Fifth Estate

The Legacy of Quebec Indian Resident Schools
Youtube: FNQLHSSC

Canada's Darkest Secret
Youtube: Al Jazeera English
Kamloops Residential School Survivors Recall

Students Going Missing
Youtube: The Fifth Estate

We Know the Truth:
Stories to Inspire Reconciliation
Youtube: CBC News

Stolen Children
Youtube: CBC News, The National

I was taken from my home; raised Jewish but Indigenous
Youtube: CBC Docs

Why Hiding Indigenous Identity May
Be a Matter of Survival
Youtube: Colorin Colorado

Why a Student Hid His Indigenous Identity
Youtube: Colorin Colorado

Quick Facts: Film 1
Luke Talks Aborigninal Identity
Youtube: Black Yarns Powered by Girraway
Survivors of Residential Schools
Youtube: BBC News
Former Residential School Child-Care Workers
Youtube: CBC News

PREDATOR PRIESTS – Ch. 6
The Case of the Predator Priest:
Abuse & Scandal in Catholic Church 2019
Youtube: CNN

Pedophilia Scandals: French Catholic Church Pleads
Forgiveness
Youtube: France 24 English

I Uncovered Abuse in The Catholic Church.
Why was it ignored?
Youtube: The New York Times

WATER CONTAMINATION – Ch. 11
Feds questioned about Global News Investigation
On First Nations Reserve
Youtube: Global News

Nations still without clean Drinking Water
Youtube: Global News
Ottawa to Investigate Long Standing Boil Water
Advisory at Neskatanga First Nation (25 yrs)
Youtube: Human Rights Watch

Attawapiskat Declares State of Emergency
Water Quality
Youtube: CBC News

Ottawa Admits it Will Miss Target to Provide
Clean Drinking Water in First Nations
Youtube: CPAC

Around 8,000 People Experience Drinking Water
Crisis in Canada ($9.00 per bottle)
Youtube: WION

SEWAGE IN LAKE ONTARIO – Ch. 5
Toronto Told to Tell Public When Untreated Sewage
Sent into Lake Ontario
Website: https://thestar.com

Toronto Flooding: Partially Treated Wastewater
Dumped into Lake Ontario
Website: https://www.toronto.ctvnews.ca

WHITE BUFFALO WOMAN - Ch. 9
A Lakota Story Connecting Heaven and Earth
Youtube: Mythos & Logos

CREATOR'S GARDEN – Ch. 10
Youtube: Joseph Pitawanakwat

FAMILY mentioned (grandparents, parents, aunts, uncles, cousins) are now all deceased as of 2015.

www.ingramcontent.com/pod-product-compliance
Lightning Source LLC
LaVergne TN
LVHW020518230925
821705LV00042B/991
* 9 7 9 8 8 9 5 4 3 0 6 6 8 *